Life

Lockdown

2020

Behind Closed Doors

Dee Bailey

Life Inna Lockdown 2020

Behind Closed Doors

Lead Author, Dee Bailey
©Simply Deez events 2020
Cover Design: Marcia M Publishing House

Edited by Marcia M Publishing House Editorial and The Write Companion Published by Marcia M Spence of Marcia M Publishing House, West Bromwich, West Midlands the UNITED KINGDOM B71 1JB

The lead authors and the co-authors assert the moral right to be identified as the author of this work

MARCIA M
PUBLISHING HOUSE

www.marciampublishing.com

Acknowledgements

In times like these, you need selfless individuals who give of themselves; their time, their resources, to support their community and beyond. They are special people who are adept at communication, whether it be spoken or unspoken. They are approachable, kind, and really care about what happens in the community, but more specifically, what is happening to individuals within it.

Bearing this in mind, I would like to express massive thanks and show appreciation for that person who is Dee Bailey.

Founder of Simply Deez Events, 'Real Talk' Radio Show Presenter and Creator of 'Life Inna Lockdown' online Zoom weekly meeting.

Dee is a fantastic organiser with what seems to be boundless energy. When I shared my idea of creating a publication to capture our stories and why, Dee did not hesitate, embraced the idea, and the rest is, well, in your hands. Thank you, Dee Bailey, for supporting a dream that is turning into a reality. We extend our gratitude.

Thank you, Shelley, aka Michelle Titmus, for your technical 'savvy' when it came to Zoom facilitation. It would not have been such a success without you.

I would also like to thank every author who has contributed to this book; the Life Inna Lockdown family, who initially loved the idea and within a few weeks had written and submitted their pieces. These authors, along with Dee, and I included, have shared, laughed, shed tears, and supported each other in many ways during this time. The result is this wonderful collaborative work. There is so much more I could add but to expedite time I will not.

Thank you so much to the Life Inna Lockdown authors!

We thank our families and friends for their support, cups of tea, wine, snacks, encouragement and patience. We love and appreciate you.

Extra special acknowledgement goes to Marcia M Spence, CEO of Marcia M Publishing House. Thank you so very much, Marcia M Spence, for your sponsorship. We appreciate it greatly.

Thank you to the National Lottery for contributing to this community initiative.

Veronica Ebanks on behalf of all co-authors

Contents

Foreword

Life Inna Lockdown : Behind Closed Doors

Never in our dreams or imaginations would any one of these authors, including me, have anticipated what was ahead of us as Big Ben's long-arm struck 12. We wished our loved ones and friends a Happy New Year 2020. I am sure that this collective of twenty-two women had not planned to have their words in print in an anthology of personal stories.

This is an important book for many reasons, but mainly because it has recorded history, an unprecedented event called Lockdown! It rolls easily off our tongues now after 12 weeks, it has become everyday language, akin to when our elders say during World War II, we are now speaking about Lockdown. This book gives you a sneak peek into what happens behind the closed doors of the authors' homes when on Lockdown March to May 2020.

I would like to commend all of the co-authors for their contribution to creating such a significant publication. I have been envigored and excited by the zeal of the Lead author Dee Bailey and Veronica Ebanks who initially planted the seed of an idea in Dee and then as Dee Bailey does, she provides the compost for the seed to grow rapidly.

It is an honour and privilege to be the publisher and a sponsor of this book, which signifies another success for Simply Deez Events.

Congratulations to all

Marcia M

Marcia M Spence
Multiple Award-Winning Author, Publisher, Woman of Influence.
CEO of Marcia M Publishing House and Academy

Introduction by Dee Bailey

Simply Deez Events began back in 2014 when I started to step out and organise my own events and create something special. Over the years, we have introduced International Women's & Men's Day Events, Health & Wellbeing and The Black Bookcase. Simply Deez Events #Lifeinnalockdown book is an anthology of written pieces, poems and journals by 22 women who have been brought together on a weekly Zoom call during the lockdown period.

It has been an opportunity to dive into our personal thoughts and space.

Vee Ebanks had the vision for this book.

"I felt we should create a publication to capture, crystalise and document our individual journeys of 'Life Inna Lockdown.' I felt this book would provide a piece of history, a snapshot in time of our lived experiences, our feelings our hopes and dreams.

I strongly believe our stories will provide a strong historical reference of this time and may provide schools, colleges and communities with valuable legacy."

When in the future people ask what happened during the Lockdown of 2020, our book will provide historical truths and insights."

The ladies had just under 3 weeks with a very tight deadline to produce their written piece as we wanted the book to be produced as soon as possible.

Who knew a weekly Zoom call would lead to some amazing friendships and women finding hidden talents! Some of these talents were already there and just needed nurturing. This journey has been a rollercoaster ride! Lots of fun, tears of joy, sorrow and hope along the way.

The Covid-19 Lockdown of March 2020 has brought out so many emotions in all of us, and we are grateful to be given this opportunity to share a snapshot in time with you.

Dee Bailey
Founder of Simply Deez Events - #Lifeinnalockdown

Chapter 1 – Veronica Ebanks

A Grandma's Take

I was excited. "I am going to be sixty this year," I proclaimed at the start of 2020. When asked by my loving husband and sons what I would like for my birthday, I shared my wish list, a party, a cruise and a nice beaded handbag.

I was going to take my side business to another level; revisiting my business plan. I had such a smart, methodical vision of how I would grow my brand. After all, I had attended so many courses around marketing and such. I even considered doing a relaunch in London.

By the beginning of March, my training contracts were few and far between, but I still had the pleasure of caring for one of my grandsons twice a week. We would go to a Music Bugs session one day and children's gym the next. When the Lockdown started, this stopped abruptly, and how do you explain this to a two-and-a-half-year-old? In fact, as an only child, it meant he would be away from other children for an unforeseen period, just like our other grandchildren who had no siblings to play with...yet.

"Mum, Dad, we are having a baby," was the news we had received in triplicate in 2019 and these 3 babies were due slap bang in the middle of this Lockdown! What were the risks to them going into hospital when all we heard was daily death figures in hospitals and then later in care homes too? Sadly, there were deaths of people we knew; our friends, as well as near misses and that, was traumatic!

I felt very protective of my sons and their wives at this time. We stayed in our house and they in theirs. We communicated via WhatsApp and Skype videos. We never had to scramble for toilet rolls as many did, as we are bulk shoppers normally and had enough sanitiser and alcohol wipes too.

Now, reader, you are probably thinking this is all about grandbabies. It isn't. Please read on.

As I write this, I am heartbroken that several days ago video footage of a Minneapolis policeman, kneeling on the neck of a man called George Floyd, was trending on social media and newsreels globally. After eight minutes of being knelt upon, George was pronounced dead when he arrived at the hospital. We heard on the TV news that the perpetrator and three other policemen who were at the scene were sacked. It took three days for charges of murder to be brought against the perpetrator following three days and nights of protests which have now spread across the United States.

I have been attending Zoom meetings throughout this time to discuss why there seems to be a disparity in numbers of Black Afro Caribbean, Asian and Ethnic minority deaths compared to that of White deaths. I listened to speakers from other countries and to groups who were raising awareness of what is happening on their continents and the suggestions and solutions for when we all emerge from Lockdown. We need a new normal.

The general narrative being theorised is that the disparity is indicative of underlying health conditions, poverty, working environments and a disregard of risk by institutions and decision-makers plus an unwillingness to speak up by Black Afro Caribbean, Asian and Ethnic minorities about the lack of Personal Protective Equipment (PPE). The first doctors who died were not impoverished. They could not all have had underlying health conditions, and when checking statistics from other continents and islands, the findings differed.

We are left with many unanswered questions, and I feel that Black Afro Caribbean, Asian and Ethnic minorities are the ones being blamed for their plight in the northern hemisphere. Some will say George Floyd was to blame for his own death. I have seen these comments before in other cases, and it angers and saddens me at the same time. Racism and hatred are still alive even at this time. Here is a poem I wrote about this three years ago:

Veronica Ebanks

'Knee'

When Colin Kaepernick, knelt down, took a knee,
He was kneeling in protest, against the murder of black
men see
He was not able to honour and revere a country where
public servants
are free,
to slay melanin-rich humanity

Number 45 has encouraged, permitted even praised
hate
More innocent humans abused and attacked to date

I am hoping and praying if, and when, they come for me
You will do something, anything, will you help me?

Martin Luther King said something like
When it is all over, it is not the voices of our enemies
that we will
Remember but the silence of our friends

Will you try to save me? Do something in solidarity
Say something about injustice and liberty

Even simply taking a knee

© Veronica Ebanks

Life Inna Lockdown 2020

During this Lockdown I have had a few days where I almost, almost, sought sanctuary by remaining in my bed all day, but I resisted and got up and lived!

In conclusion, we cannot be onlookers in the face of injustice and hate. George Floyd wanted to live! I have cried, signed petitions and I am hopeful that justice will be done, and that peace, equity and unity will be the 'new normal' across the world.

I hope and pray our three beautiful granddaughters (I can't wait to cradle them in my arms), born in the midst of this Lockdown will be, if not loved, but protected, by those who do not look like them and that they will be treated humanely, afforded dignity, respect and allowed to live!

This is something I wish for every single person reading this.

I am a spiritual person and truly full of gratitude for everything; my family, friends, my life, co-workers, opportunities, gifts and the Simply Deez crew. My side business plans are delayed but not destroyed.

I will not go on the planned cruise this year but may have a small family party for my 60th birthday. Oh, and I hope that I do get a nice beaded handbag.

About Veronica Ebanks BSc MFHT

An Afro-Caribbean lady from Jamaica via London, Veronica is now resident in the Midlands. She has been married to Al for 38 years with four sons and eleven grandchildren.

Veronica has a Science and Education past work history. After redundancy she created a career for herself as an Independent Safeguarding Consultant/Trainer/ Restorative Justice Practitioner and Entrepreneur. She is the founder of Verelba Mind & Body (VMB), a skincare, wellbeing and holistic therapy brand.

Putting her head above the parapet to share her poetry and writing publicly, she debuted in performance poetry in February 2016 at the 'X Marks the Spot' Showcase in Bedfordshire.

Veronica also volunteers with Friends of the Caribbean Charity in Milton Keynes, and she has a love for people, literature, theatre, singing, gardening and vintage clothing.

11

Chapter 2 – Theresa Rhodes

What do you really see?

What things did I really take notice of before the Covid-19 2020 Lockdown?

Not much really as I was always busy doing things and meeting up with many people to bother. How much time was I giving to myself and the things I enjoyed? I am not sure as I was always doing loads of things to please others like volunteering at the hospital and looking after my mum. Yes, I really love helping people, but did I really know who I was as a person? Was I giving myself enough space? These are interesting questions asked with hindsight.

Before the Lockdown, my life was busy with classes, social groups, volunteering plus work and caring for my mum. Never a day went by when I didn't meet up with many people, and I felt that my life was happy. I attended church on a Sunday and occasionally during the week and joined in some church activities. Little did I know that things were about to change!

It was the middle of March, and the news was not looking good. A virus that had already claimed thousands of lives in China, the USA and several places in Italy became prevalent in the UK.

The Prime Minister, Boris Johnson, announced on Monday, 13 March, that by Saturday, 21 March, people with certain health conditions like myself would need to go into our houses and shield ourselves from the outside world, for 12 weeks as this virus was spreading rapidly and we were in danger.

Being a Roman Catholic, the first thing I thought about on the following Sunday morning was the fact that on the previous Friday I had been to the last Mass for some time at the church, and we had all said goodbye to each other, wishing each other well, not knowing when we would see each other again. It was a strange feeling. It was then I decided that I would find a Mass that I could watch, either on the TV or through the internet, and make it part of my daily routine.

So, for the rest of the Lockdown, I tried to keep to this routine as well as attending prayer times and retreats. It was the main thing for me, and it kept me strong.

On Sundays and special days, I invited the elderly lady that I normally take to church, to join me and listen in via the telephone to the mass and so we continued to pray together through the Lockdown.

At first, it was strange not going out, but surprisingly something started to happen in my life. I started to become calmer and more in control of things.

I started to look around my house and see things in a new light. Before the Lockdown, I had not been one to spend much time at home and at times didn't really like the house for a number of reasons. However, as the days turned into weeks and then months, I came to love my house! It was my haven of safety and peace.

I started to cook more. Before we used to get things out of the freezer and put them in the oven or in a pan. As I started experimenting, I loved to make dishes such as stir-fries, different pasta dishes, stuffed vegetables and other simple but tasty meals. It's a good job we both love fruit and vegetables as I soon started to notice I was feeling a little heavier than previously because I was not as active.

The garden became a joy! It is amazing what you see when you just look. I spent time just looking at the different colour of leaves in the hedge; the way a fly or a butterfly looked close up and other beautiful things. Bluebells in the garden brought a touch of spring, and my husband gave me the best Easter present, as he showed me a beautiful clump of red tulips that he had grown in a pot in the garden. God was certainly working in my life.

Things were not always easy as I knew there were tragedies all around. The news continued to provide upsetting updates, and sadly we lost our beloved aunt to the virus.

At times I felt the longing to go to a shop or go for a walk. I just wanted to do something "normal" again. I did 'escape' a couple of times, including on the 1 May, when I woke up early and went for a walk by a local river to see the sunrise and hear the dawn chorus. There was no one about, so I felt safe. But we also had disappointment as our holiday was cancelled.

As I can see my day of freedom in sight, there is one thing that I have missed above everything, and that is seeing my mother. That first glimpse of her, face to face, will be the greatest gift that no money can buy, and I will make her the first person I see on the outside of this Lockdown. I hope that all people will have the same experience when they meet their loved ones again.

I pray that this virus can be truly eradicated and that people will continue with their acts of kindness to others. I know that I will continue to value the little things in life. I will cherish the new friendships I have made with neighbours that I have never spoken to before but have stopped and chatted with when I was in my garden watching the world go by and marvelling at God's creation.

About Theresa Rhodes

I have been happily married to Peter for 35 years, and through this time of Lockdown, we have become closer than ever. My sister and two brothers have also been at the end of the phone. My elderly mum is amazing.

I am a personal assistant to a lovely lady who I have kept in touch with during this time, and we have shared many happy conversations and look forward to meeting again to go to the hobby club and for walks.

As a lover of words, I write poetry and belong to a poetry society. I have published a poetry book which raises money for charity. I am also a member of Toastmasters International, where I can join with others who are eager to increase their speaking and leadership skills. Throughout my adult life, I have been a volunteer, and this gives me great satisfaction.

Chapter 3 – Stephanie Powell

I Thought I was Already There

My life in the Covid-19 2020 lockdown began way, way before 'Life Inna Lockdown' started.

For me, I already felt I was in Lockdown because of the current situation I was already living in.

In March 2020, the official, UK wide lockdown began in England is still ongoing...

Lockdown can have a very different meaning to us all. What does Lockdown mean to you? It has meant the following to me:

- Having to stop the things you enjoy doing but not through your own choice

- Dealing with illness and mental health problems

- Change which is out of your control

- Loss of control within your home

- No choice and unable to have an opinion in a working environment

- Unable to have an opinion and not being heard because your voice doesn't count

- A disability that stops you from achieving your goals

- Loss of control over your own life

- Others trying to control you

- Loss of independence that you were used to

This occurs when things are not what you decided or chose but continue for longer then you expected.

I feel Lockdown may well have started during childhood for me and through my growing up years too, but without me realising.

For example, through life-style experiences:

- Social situations

- Workplace experiences

- Home environment

For the last three years of my life, I feel I have been in Lockdown on a roundabout. One minute I am trying to get on with my life and the next I am at a standstill, unable to do anything.

During the latter end of last year, my body was in complete Lockdown. My life has changed suddenly from being a very active, outgoing person, to be more homebound, although not through choice. I have had to enlist the help of others to do just some of the simple things within the home and in my daily life.

Some days, my body has done a complete 360-degree turn on me, shutting down with one problem after another and not allowing me to do anything at all at times. This has come with tears, anger, pain, frustration, stress, worry and the tension of knowing this is not truly me.

As if this was not enough, 'Life Inna Lockdown' began for all of us in the country, in every household, so having time and space on my own at home changed too.

Isolation began as I and others in the home were showing signs of the virus, Covid-19. This was a worrying time for us all. I was fearful for my life as there were so many things going on.

As the isolation countdown started at fourteen days, I was hoping and praying everything would be OK and that things would turn around. Trying to stay in a positive mindset has got me this far, being grateful for each day, wanting to get on with things that I had planned to do but sometimes accepting I had no energy to get things done.

I would try to bring my own sunshine and happiness whilst stuck indoors, reflecting and still trying to continue to find the positive in the negative whilst trying to work towards my goals, which my body really wasn't allowing at all.

This came with more stress on top of stress because of a member of my family was having to put themselves in danger by going out to get basic items needed, as there was no chance of booking an online supermarket delivery slot for weeks.

Those moments were worrying times with a lot of 'what if's' going on. As the saying goes 'It never rains, but it pours'. Believe me, it has certainly been 'pouring' for my family of late and me!

I was also enduring a lack of sleep which had been affecting me for months before the Lockdown too, plus a loss of appetite because of how I was feeling.

Planned medical appointments were having to be changed and rescheduled because of the current virus situation. All I wanted were answers to my own health situation so that I could move on with my life.

Some tough times I have had, but for me, this lockdown situation has topped it all; as I write we are in the ninth week of Lockdown, isolated with my family, not feeling my strongest, positive, optimistic self.

I haven't seen any of my extended family for months on end, and I am feeling like I have no breathing space anymore.

As the days linger on, I do feel blessed to be alive, but things are getting harder as my patience is wearing out and with each other.

I have realised the things I took for granted. I have not had any affection being shown to me since the Lockdown began and loneliness has kicked in even though there are others in the home. We have tried to show each other respect and give each other space.

Early morning became golden to me 'like a breath of fresh air' before the day began in the silence of my home. I had to do what helped me through. We were not used to being cooped up together twenty-four-seven, but during this time, there has also been family bonding with things being done in different ways because things had to change.

I am hoping and praying that my life will have a big turnaround now, allowing me to follow the path I am dreaming of and more.

Major changes I endure, with things looking like they can move to a whole new level; a time when I am able to follow my dreams. I feel the world will become a different place after Lockdown because of the way we will do things in the future.

For me, it is about what I have learnt through life's journey and experiences of others and how they cope and deal with life. We see people taking platforms that are available during times of crisis, but why do we wait till then?

I feel I have become much stronger, especially during my tough times. Self-doubt is what has helped me through to prove a point to me. It doesn't mean you are weaker than anybody else.

About Stephanie Powell.

Stephanie is married with one son, and she has worn numerous hats in life so far!

She first dabbled with creative writing in her mid-twenties, yet only wrote pieces for special occasions.

Stephanie has had years of experience working in a professional sector, helping different generations develop.

Over the last two years she decided to rekindle previous hobbies having had to push them aside because of a lack of time. This was due to leading a hectic and unbalanced life.

Having led a quiet and successful life overall, Stephanie has endured some difficulties along the way and reached a point where she began soul-searching.

Ultimately, the direction she wishes to work towards is slowly being put into action, so watch this space!

Chapter 4 – Michelle Titmus

Embracing Change

The date is 7 March 2020, and we have had an amazing day celebrating International Women's Day with the Simply Deez Events team. All through the day there is concerned chatter about the Covid-19 virus that has started in China. At first, everyone I had spoken to had been upset for those that had died but not too concerned as it's all happening on the other side of the world.

Not much information has been released by the Chinese authorities although I have seen an online press conference from some experts in the medical field who couldn't explain the virus well, as they couldn't get the information they need about the virus; the infection rate, how it's transmitted, etc.

Little did we know that this would be one of the last weekends that felt normal.

I had already arranged to go and visit my Mum the following week as she lives in Weymouth, which is a journey from where I live.

This would be a welcome time out for me from the chaos recently and would be the last weekend that dogs would be allowed on all parts of the beach (Easter weekend marks the start of visitor season and dogs are only allowed on certain parts of the beach until the Autumn half term.)

On the days that followed, we heard that the virus had spread to other countries including France. This was a lot closer to the United Kingdom where we are and still there wasn't a full explanation about the virus, or any plans of how to stop the spreading or the best course of action moving forward.

Not knowing what was to come didn't help my conversations with what Mum needed and how I was to leave her, as we live in the Bedfordshire area. It had also brought up memories for my Mum, as the nearest thing 'quarantine' has meant for her was when the debilitating disease Polio was around when she was a child. She remembers not being able to attend school, and people had to stay in their own back gardens in the fresh air.

I have hosted a Facebook live broadcast from the beach explaining how TJ and I are saying goodbye to the beach until the Autumn, and we had no clue just how much meaning that goodbye would hold.

Ever since that weekend, I have felt like I have been in a whirlwind; some days only hanging on by my fingertips.

I have my own baking business which has been put on hold pretty much. Social distancing and no contact deliveries are a bit difficult, and parties have been cancelled.

I am a Trustee at a charity called Families United Network. We provide respite care for children and young adults with additional needs. We have had to close our building and services to protect our children and staff.

My other charity and community work mean the usual events or gatherings have to be cancelled.

However, it has meant we have discovered new ways of bringing everyone together; things we have never thought of before, or something we had planned to possibly do yet never did, and the Lockdown has handed that opportunity and need to do it.

I have been using the time to gain as much knowledge as I can. I have been taking lots of training and Zoom calls for both personal and business use. New baking courses mean new goodies to offer when I can open my baking business again.

Learning and training about mental health and suicide prevention is a personal project and calling of mine and I have been able to learn and absorb, ultimately passing on my knowledge to the communities I am involved with.

This is all thanks to the OLLIE Foundation providing online free or reduced-price courses, all of which have been modified for a quick turnaround as no training had ever been available online before. This is something I had heard other charities mention and had discovered they had delivered successfully.

F. U. N. has turned on its head and is providing care virtually, and as I write this, we have set up a plan to open our respite care service with lots of Personal Protection Equipment (PPE), a cleaning rota and one-to-one childcare.

My mum has worked on her laptop and found the links to local church services in order to keep in touch.

But of course, something I am really proud of is setting up the weekly Zoom calls with Simply Deez Events 'Life Inna Lockdown'.

When your Sista has a heart-to-heart with you about our community and what we can do to support each other (like we do with the Ladies Soirées), the weekly Zoom calls began, and I had to learn a new media tool in a very short space of time.

As quite often happens, the unconscious 'Deez Effect' has taken these events onto another level, which brings like-minded people together and organically mentors and cares for all involved. It's a wonderful thing but difficult to explain the feeling.

So here we are at the end of May 2020, and to look forward to the future is a very difficult thing to get your head around.

There are people I know that have died of the virus. I know people who have had to cancel events like weddings. Babies have been born during the Lockdown and haven't been able to be welcomed into the family with the usual cuddles and celebrations.

Not seeing close family and friends and hugging, which is a huge thing for me, has been difficult. I personally should have been attending one of the Queen's Garden Parties with my Mum due to my volunteer work, but this had to be cancelled.

My own mental health has put a strange slant on my feelings about Lockdown. I could say I have had times of self-isolation myself many times over the years. All I can say is "It's Ok to not be Ok" and if you need to take a day, when you go out into the 'real world' it will take it out of you more than you would think. Be kind to yourself and others.

Most importantly reach out. Everyone needs help sometimes, so please listen (and properly listen) to those around you and share how you are feeling if you need help. Nothing is too silly or too difficult to overcome. You may just need someone other than yourself to work out whatever it is that is bothering you.

Take time. Who knows when or where this will take us? Try to find a positive one day at a time.

About Michelle (Shelley) Titmus

Michelle is a wife, and mum to a 'fur baby,' her dog TJ. She is an auntie to many and a third-generation Lutonian from a very large family.

She owns and runs a bakery business called Shelley Scrumptious and is known as the 'Mad Baker.'

She is a volunteer at Deez Events and a Trustee at Families United Network, a SEND children's and young adults respite support charity.

Shelley is also a volunteer on the Relay for Life - Luton for Cancer Research UK Committee and a supporter for the OLLIE Foundation in Bedfordshire which is a charity that provides training in the prevention of suicide, suicide awareness, intervention, and mental wellbeing.

Chapter 5 – Sandra Moore

Moore Free Time

Hibernary

I decided that January 2020 was going to be my month of hibernation; using the month to plan my successes for the coming year and relishing the festive leftovers. I never understood the madness of December, the big party on the 31st and then flipping the switch at the stroke of midnight, making up countless resolutions to either become a new person or do things differently without the staying power; basically going from one hundred miles per hour to zero. So, I planned my new year to start on the 1 February and off I went. My health and wellbeing side hustle was taking off and then…

The COVID-19 virus situation was hitting the news, gathering momentum from east to west, north to south. I was taking notice and started alerting my clients. There were mixed messages about how it was going to affect our lives and the economies of the world; there was also complacency.

On reflection, I don't think any of us realised the impact that this was going to have on our daily lives, and our grief at the loved ones that we would lose, not just from the COVID-19 virus but of terminal illnesses, accidents, natural causes and literally dying from a broken heart.

My job affords me the flexibility to work from home, and in February I worked more from home than I had in any one month prior, partly because I was not feeling a hundred per cent well, and partly due to the travelling and the continuous disruptions of the trains, but mostly because we had received news that my father was in the final stages of life. I sensed something big was looming not just from the pending loss of my father but because I could see a veil on the horizon coming closer and closer to cover us all.

On the days I went into the office I was getting annoyed with the lack of decorum people exhibited when travelling on the train and tube, coughing without covering their mouths and the general lack of awareness of peoples' personal space. I'm not sure why I had even noticed this more than I normally would. After all, that was the general behaviour of some people which we have come to accept in our society, or maybe not accept but tolerate, or maybe just letting it absorb into the ether without batting an eyelid anymore.

One morning after the now expected train delays and crowded compartments, I was walking through St Pancras to catch the tube when out of nowhere a voice in my head said 'I want more free time and a six-figure income'. I did not realise how close I was to getting part of that desire come true.

Lockdown – More Free Time

I felt excited about the 'more free time' that was to come! I was looking forward to getting my website completed, reading, exercising, finishing my online course, getting jobs in the house and garden started and finished; binge-watching Netflix; the list went on and on and on.

I felt apprehensive as my income was going to be impacted; the company where I worked was going to close as most of our clients went into Lockdown. I had a choice. I could worry about something I couldn't change, or I could turn this into a positive experience. Positivity won… initially.

On the 2 April, I recorded a radio interview for Derby Local Radio on mental health and wellbeing, signposting names and phone numbers of organisations that could offer support. I was feeling good! I felt that I had made a small yet positive contribution to help those in Lockdown. And then…

A phone call came from my sister to say that my dad's breathing had changed. Mum, my sister, my brother and I spent the last few hours of his life together. His body decided the time had come to rest, and so his final release of breath was at 2:30 pm. We were in the unique situation of being together; the COVID-19 virus had taken this precious moment away from many others. We were and are thankful that we were allowed this gift. Psalm 23 'The Lord is My Shepherd…'

Rest in Eternal Peace

We were only allowed to have immediate family members at my dad's funeral, but because he was well-loved and appreciated, there were many well-wishers waiting outside the house who all clapped as the hearse pulled away. On arrival at the cemetery, his 'gate-crashers' appeared - all social distancing. He had obviously made an impact on their lives.

A Surreal Moment in Time

Negativity was creeping in...I felt cocooned in a myriad of emotions, skyrocketing into the heavens then falling into the earth's belly; lounging in bed, eating whatever, then berating myself for having one too many cakes or biscuits or a large slice of butter on my toast; binge-watching Netflix then berating myself for wasting time, sadness and tears, joy and laughter of childhood memories; Zoom meetings, webinars; then panic that I was not exercising or meditating or practising my Qi Gong or cleaning the house or weeding the garden. Fear was setting in that I was wasting my 'more free time' and I was not being gentle with myself, I was being HARD! I spoke to a dear friend, and she said, "It is ok not to be ok." I already knew this; this is what I say to others, so why not to me? Positivity waved, and I waved back!

I started walking in nature, discovering the true beauty of where I had lived for 28 years! I took charge of my mental health and wellbeing and for once did not feel guilty whilst truly appreciating Mother Earth's healing arms.

Nature's Beauty

Heady perfume smells of blossoms with the
buzz of the bees
Birds tweeting and chirping in their
musical chorus line
Dancing of the leaves to the sweet
overtures of the wind
Majestic trees reaching to heaven
Rolling green hills of ancient times
Timeless healing of Mother's arms

About Sandra Moore

Sandra started out as a Registered General Nurse before retraining and qualifying as a Chartered Environmental Health Practitioner with over 30 years' experience in food safety and health and safety.

Sandra is also passionate about health and wellness issues and is a Health and Wellbeing Consultant. She launched her wellbeing business in Autumn 2019. Rejuvenated Soul specialises in meditation, sound, colour and energy therapies.

Another of Sandra's loves is designing and printing t-shirts, mugs, journals and other merchandise. She is also a novice photographer and loves to travel, read, cook, walk, cycle and binge-watch good dramas. In 2018 at the age of

55, she trekked one of the Inca Trails which was 4800m above sea level, and she considers this to be one of her greatest achievements.

She has three sons and two granddaughters who she absolutely adores.

Chapter 6 – Nike Akiti

My Search for Flour & Other Tales of Choosing Happiness

*Faith is the substance of things hoped for, the evidence of things unseen...*Hebrews 11:1

In the lead, up to the 2020 lockdown, my life was not particularly spectacular or groovy, but it was *my* non-spectacular, non-groovy life and it is a part of the Lockdown; the stories of curtailed freedom, food scarcity, and humanity at its highest and lowest.

I had just come back from a holiday in Morocco, and I was training for a sponsored weight lift (which I just about managed to get done) going to work, going to Zumba, shopping and doing normal everyday things. I was ok, but the murmurs were getting louder;

strange things were happening in places around the world, and then on the 23 March we were told the virus was here. My volunteer commitments were out of the window, and we were told to stay home. In one fell swoop life was changed.

Online had become less sexy and the place where everyday life was happening. Zoom, FaceTime, WhatsApp, Microsoft Teams, and so many other programs and apps; who knew? I am not going to lie, I thought the Lockdown would pass pretty much the same way as the SARS situation did, but reports kept getting gloomier and gloomier, and I sometimes became just a little fearful.

My Lockdown consists of extra time with my husband! Sharing silly giggles and the joint moans about this and that. His work dried up instantly, but I'm working from home.

In the beginning, when shopping, I had to search for eggs as they were so scarce. It was at this point my friend, and I doubled up and shopped for each other, restrictions allowing of course. We are on lockdown Day 69 now, and so it continues. I did not understand the panic buying, and until today I still don't understand the obsession with buying toilet roll. In my opinion, it defied logic!

My work IT system was extremely temperamental, and sometimes it could take up to an hour to come on even after with multiple attempts. On 1 April, I was already feeling out of sorts and had my first real negative moment, and then it took 55 minutes to log back on after lunch. It felt weird. I was home, but it felt like I wasn't.

For some inexplicable reason, I was obsessed with flour, especially wholemeal. It was so hard to come by, and I knew this, yet no matter what shop I was in, I'd go to the flour section to have a nosy. Then, I randomly went into a shop I hardly ever go into on the town's High Street, and they had Nigerian wheatflour, which I know to be wholemeal. Result!

The next day I was in Morrisons supermarket and on my visit to the flour aisle there were two bags of wholemeal bread flour! Flour it seems has turned into a bus! So, I gifted my friend Meze a bag of flour.

I, like the rest of the nation, had found bread-making my new treat at the weekend and there was none of this proofing here, kneading there, leave to rest, etc…for me. Nope! Two ingredients and less than an hour for the whole process!

It pained me, not seeing my family, my friends; I have not seen my new baby great nephew since he was born just before I went to Morocco.

I haven't seen my niece and nephew (another set) for just as long, and during the religious celebration of Eid, I had the hopeful notion that I might see them, but it was just a pipe dream. I feel deeply now, more than previously, and I notice my lack of direct offspring. They do say you regret the things you haven't done, not the things you have! Another story, another place.

I decided early on that I was not buying into any conspiracy theories and would limit watching the news. I wasn't interested in the blame game. After all, it doesn't matter who spills the milk, it still needs to be cleaned up! I followed the guidelines set out by the government and left everything else to faith. I've had two mini meltdowns and more than a few blue moments. I don't know if it's the reflections or the projections, but that is how it has been for me.

A lack of freedom has been a big thing too. I, for one initially felt curtailed. I couldn't find the things I needed, but upon reflection, I realised I was just asked to do my bit for the greater good.

I was still free to do nothing, eat rubbish and watch dumb TV, or I could take a positive attitude and make the best (there is a best) of the choices I make.

I have really felt grateful for my blessings, my husband, my family, my sister-friends and my extended family by virtue of my extracurricular activities, and I must not forget my online community. All my extra activities transitioned online, hence a realisation of how much I do; not a moment was spare, except luckily, I gained the travel time back. I never thought of myself as one who would exercise at home, but here I am, doing just that on Zoom and on Facebook live. This happened on 3 April. There was a Ladies Soiree on Zoom; I stopped what I was doing to do Tae Kwon Do on Facebook live; most of the country stopped to clap for the NHS on a Thursday evening; then I went back onto the Soiree; did my own Facebook live, and then in the morning there was Bootcamp exercise on Zoom! It was, and continues to be, a Zoom epidemic! (Wow! I should have bought shares in that company!)

As much as I miss the social outings, I've realised I'm equally a happy home buddy. I've found a 'Mrs Mop' inside me that I didn't even know existed. My dishwasher has been reborn, and my car is hanging on for dear life, aided by my taking it out for a drive every day. In the beginning, this was a joy; a little bit of defiance even, but now it's a chore.

My point really, is acceptance of what I could not change, empathy and encouragement for others, and in everything I give thanks to God.

About Nike Akiti (aka) Msnikkidee

I am a happiness champion on a mission to help people choose health and happiness by beating the faddy diet blues and practising self-care and love. My name is Nike Akiti aka Msnikkidee

I hail from Luton. I am a child of Nigerian parents and the wife of Dennis. I love people, but not naysayers. I want to go everywhere and wish I could have met Nelson Mandela. I am scared of not making a difference but dream of showing people it's never too late to follow their dreams. I am determined the world will be a happier place.

I value freedom, good health and good relationships. I am proud of becoming a Black Belt in Tae Kwon Do and very happy to have mastered my workout ethic; I'm a Zumba lover!

Chapter 7 – Daniela Svampa Cowie

No Human Touch

As a voice in business and my daily expression, to bring hope, love and strength to every life who crosses my path, I have worked and still work every day to spread the message that nothing is insurmountable and I feel this to be of paramount importance more today than in the past. I am a great believer that a smile, a compliment, a word of encouragement and a hug goes a long way to enrich the life of another being.

Before the Lockdown, I have been able to do this on a very personal level and loved every moment of it, every touch, every hug, every exchange. I am a people person and in the personal approach, as a 'present' being, is when I believe I am at my best. It's my comfort zone.

When the Covid-19 virus hit the UK, and we had to enter Lockdown, for me, already used to working from home, nothing much really changed, yet at the same time, all did.

A seemingly contradictory statement, but true none the less. Whilst being used to meeting and dealing with my clients face to face in the comfort of my own home, and delivering talks to audiences with a tangible presence, everything has now switched to online; for me, an interaction I have always felt to be cold and detached.

I must confess, I have always had a bit of an issue with the usage of technology, and I have spent most of my life resisting it, but as the saying goes 'what we resist persists'.

I think this pandemic has brought different lessons for each one of us according to where we are in our life, so perhaps for me, one of the main lessons has been to see the beauty and benefit of the technological world.

I believe in gratitude being one of the major factors in the enrichment of our lives, and yet this was one aspect in our world that I was not applying it to. I never saw the 'gem' in it. It is thanks to this very thing

I have resisted and honestly cursed so much in the past, that I have been able to keep my world moving.

I can still speak and see my son who is still in his university accommodation miles away from me; I can still help people; I can still work and earn money for all of my essentials and commodities; I can even reach further afield and spread my powerful message, as through technology, distance online is of no object. This for many might be of minor importance, but for someone like me who has had a massive block over any sort of technical stuff and a reluctance to move with the new ways of the world, it is massive.

It has not been easy, and my head is still trying to adapt to this shift in certain ways, so much so that I often find it exhausting. I do enjoy and look forward to my daily walks, not so much for the good feel factor that exercise brings, but because, although I cannot reach out and hug another being or ruffle the coat of a dog, I can see them, feel their energy and exchange a warm smile rather than a digital word.

One day, hopefully in the near future, this Lockdown will lift, and society will step back into a more familiar routine, resembling more of how it used to be rather than what has been.

Life Inna Lockdown 2020

During this time of Lockdown, although it has been hard on a lot of people, whether through loss, financial or in personal struggles, I believe there have been great things too. The earth has had a chance to heal, and people have become closer and generally more supportive of one another; more considerate.

We have been reminded of the benefits of slowing down, of the importance of family, friendship, love! We have been given the opportunity to reassess our values, our priorities, our wellbeing, and what truly matters in our lives. I think a lot of us have come to see the futility of a status and the importance of each input regardless of the label; that each part played by any individual carries its worth and matters. No separation in gender, creed, religion, colour, class or status; all united in one battle.

A Poetic Reflection

Many hearts joined as one
Expressing in a myriad of ways
Journeying through this storm...
Some lost in death
Some losing themselves
Some 'holding it together'
Some seeing the gift to rediscover
All doing the best we can
Walking each other through
Walking each other home
With hope in our hearts

About Daniela Svampa Cowie

Daniela is originally from Italy and has lived in England for over half of her life. She is a wife, mother to two amazing young men and a lover of life!

Daniela is an Integrative Therapy Counsellor, an author and an Inspirational Speaker. She believes and sees the good in pretty much everything, trusting in the bigger picture and believing that everything happens for a reason.

Daniela is a survivor of trauma and has chosen to use her experiences to be of service to others in her career.

Chapter 8 – Natalie Wedderburn

A Whole New World

A whole new world has unfolded right before my eyes
This pandemic has taken me by surprise
Trying daily to separate the truth from the lies
My children ask questions from curious minds

Searching for the best explanation for this sad
situation
These rules and regulations are causing
complications

Life Inna Lockdown 2020

Limiting opportunities for play and exploration
More love, time and dedication are all I can give
Thankful I have been blessed with another day to live
Oh, how time has changed
So many things have been rearranged
This harsh reality has become the new normality
Simplicity replaced with complexity
We are no longer who we think we should be
Lockdown has made us puppets on a string
Left, right, up, down, let the show begin

Ladies and gentlemen, are you sitting tight?
This grand performance will last more than one night
Friends and family caught in the panic
A simple shopping trip turns out to be manic
Play, pause, rewind, things are just the same
The reasons, the causes, who is to blame?
Mummy, when can we go out again?
When it is over, I say and hope not in vain

And while this history is in the making
I find myself doing a lot more baking
With extra time I teach my children important lessons
When this is over these will leave lasting impressions
This time together has been an inspiration
There is no greater joy than guiding the next
generation

About Natalie Wedderburn

Natalie is a primary school teacher. She was awarded her Bachelor of Arts in Primary Education at the University of Roehampton in London.

Natalie is also a mother and the author of Be Polite, a children's picture book. Her children inspired her to write Be Polite as she is passionate about developing them into well- mannered individuals.

She hopes Be Polite will also encourage all children around the world to be respectful in their everyday lives.

Natalie home educates her children which she finds empowering and rewarding. She enjoys going shopping and listening to music in her spare time. Natalie lives in Bedfordshire with her partner and their young children.

Chapter 9 – Jannette Barrett

Sweating Like a Glassblower's Armpit

It's 5.50am, and I'm pulling up outside Mrs P's flat. She watches the Good Morning Britain programme. Why? Piers Morgan, that's why! Personally, I think he is one of the most arrogant farts on the planet, but right now, he is the only one with gumption; the only one asking the right questions and the only one pushing to get our Personal Protective Clothing (PPE) to protect us while we work as carers in the community.

Wow! To think PPE would become a nationwide topic of conversation because of a devastating shortage and catastrophic demand for it! Most people didn't even know what those initials stood for before the Covid-19 virus and then there's that other word everyone keeps saying; 'unprecedented'. If I had a pound for every time I heard that word, I'd have no problem buying my own PPE!

My goodness! What a mess we are all in and those in charge don't seem to have a clue of what to do for the best.

Being a freelance mental health practitioner, I feel as though I'm stuck in a wilderness.

Everything that's discussed seems to be about the NHS! They are not the only key workers out in the thick of it, out in the eye of the storm. It's really tough out here.

Doing any sort of community nursing or care was always tough going, but now the freelancers are definitely feeling left out, and we're all just burning out trying to do our best. Anyway, I must stop procrastinating and get myself inside.

"Morning Mrs P."

"Good morning Jan, did you bring my paper?" The same old thing: she says this every day bless her.

My husband is a merchandiser for Midlands Media and manages the daily papers, magazines and resources for the city's hotels, trains and shops and even the various TV news channels, so I can get a spare Daily Mail newspaper from him to take to her.

"Yes, I've got your mail." I always take it up to her with a cup of tea, each playing their part. Tea to stimulate the digestive tract and the paper to get the old girls brain cells functioning.

Now it's time for me to put on my PPE. Two masks, two pairs of gloves and I haven't got a gown, so I wear a light cotton pyjama jacket. It has to be something that can take a 90-degree temperature wash.

Ridiculous, I know, but that's the PPE crisis I'm afraid. I also add two plastic aprons, front and back, along with my head wrap. I already wear glasses, so I get some protection for my eye area because I haven't got a visor either.

Blooming heck, it's not easy working in it all especially with my hands; my fingers feel like Chipolata sausages, and I end up sweating like a glassblower's armpit! It's horrible. At the end of each day, it's not just my clothes that need a boil wash, I can tell you!

Imagine showering someone whilst wearing all that. The humidity alone is enough; you can't see for the steam, and your own sweat tickles your face as it rolls down. You can't touch your face, remember? Its absolute murder when all you want to do is scratch it.

I try twitching my nose, then moving my mouth around and around but nothing works. I just must bear it until I can open her window when I've completed her personal hygiene. Oh, the joy when I unhook the masks off my right ear, breathe in some clean, fresh air and start to dry off. Breathing in those masks is deadly, but there's no way I can open the window during her shower. Mrs P is 94yrs old.

When that is all done, there's yet another task that feels so different when wearing all the PPE, the dressing. My sausage fingers fumble when doing up Mrs P's buttons or tying anything so it all takes longer and it's time I haven't got.

Do you know what that means to me? No break. My time gets swallowed up, but I swallow nothing. I get dehydrated with all that gear on, not that I can readily take off my masks and eat or drink with my clients in fear of passing anything on!

Yep! It's tough out here, alright, and the government isn't getting anything right for us so far. Maybe some of Colonel Tom Moore's fundraising money will. Nah! Can't see that happening either. Not for me, anyhow, as I'm a freelance sole trader.

I'll just keep going as best I can as all my clients need me, and I'll keep sweating like a glassblower's armpit and lose some weight with the lack of food.

Something good may come from all this! A nice new size 10 outfit perhaps. Uhum! We're in a new world. I just hope and pray that all the unification, community camaraderie and family bonding continue in the aftermath and we all leave memorable legacies. 'Life Inna lockdown'. You don't know half of it!

About Jannette Barrett (aka) Ms Lyricist B

Jannette is a wife and mother of three and works as a freelance mental health community practitioner.

She is also a grandmother of three and a proud dyslexic published author. She loves to write songs, poetry and scripts.

Jannette believes the pen is a mighty implement which can be used to either endorse or destroy. With that in mind, she has always tried to adhere to a tactile balance before she shares her deepest thoughts because "any words left by me will be part of my legacy."

Chapter 10 – Rita James

This is My Never-Ending Story

5 September 2018, the day before my birthday. "Rita, you have cancer."

I laughed at the doctor and said, "Oh well, size 10 here I come."

I was in a different world. The room was so quiet. I felt I was all alone, and I was not taking anything in. My husband broke down crying. I came home and told my four children and spoke to all my family.

It was very sad as the history of my family is not good. I lost my mum and dad, plus two sisters. I thought, 'Here we go, it's my time to go.'

So October came, and the Chemotherapy treatment started. It was for 72 hours nonstop, and it was horrific. This would be every three weeks for five months. The pain and everything else that goes with cancer are unreal, and many times I cried and wanted to give up.

Then I had to have an 11.5cm tumour removed. The day they scheduled for the operation was the 1 April (aka) April Fools Day! I did laugh.

They had to remove some nerves as well and then I had to have five weeks of radiotherapy every single day. That destroyed me.

So, from 2018 to 2020, I'm still fighting to be here, but since the Covid-19 Lockdown, the situation has made me think more and generally I'm not one to show my feelings; I'll help anyone but keep how I'm feeling to myself. I'm very humbled because I have the best family in the world and many great friends and have met some new ones along the way but who would have thought meeting Dee and Shelley and to be on Zoom, that they would be the ones that make me talk of how I'm truly feeling!

When I lost my first sister, Yvonne, she was only 35 years old, and I was the only one not there when she passed, as I was on my way home from Germany. She promised to wait for me because I was only going for the weekend, but she left me a message saying, "Tell Rita, I'm sorry."

Well, that broke my heart big time for many years. I felt so guilty for not being there when she passed but we made sure her son was going to be brought up by all of us.

Then, another sister was gone, Margaret. She was everyone's mum as she could not have children, so we were her children. Every Mother's Day, we would spoil her, alongside my niece Char. Margaret was the rock of our family and, yes, this did destroy my mum, as well as all of us, but being in this Lockdown makes you think how lucky you are.

I'm not ready to go anywhere at the moment, and I want that happy ending.

I became bitter against a few, and I'll never forgive these people who I helped a lot in the past, but I wouldn't have dreamed that they could not give me a call or text or even a letter to see how I am. I feel it's their loss to lose someone like me. There are many that have said, "I want to be like Rita."

I've still got many appointments coming up in London, and I didn't know that I had got fibrosis due to all the treatments; it's no wonder why some days I can't do a thing and some days I don't want to get out of bed. I started thinking more of my mum and thought if she can cope with everything in her life, then I can get out of bed and do my best and never give up because there are many that love me and need me.

I have so many stories to tell, and that's why this piece of writing is called My Never-Ending Story. I can't thank Dee and Shelley enough and sometimes think they might regret knowing me!

I will be seeing my professors in London and I'll say, "What went wrong? Look at me! I've gone out not in. I thought chemotherapy was meant to shrink your body!" I'll always thank these nurses and doctors, even the cleaner was just as important to me.

About Rita James

Rita has been married for 32 years and has four wonderful children.

Retired from her work at Tesco due to ill health Rita is looking forward to continuing her charity work.

She is looking forward to 'ringing the bell' when her treatment for cancer ends.

It's her Never-Ending Story, and she looks forward to a happy ending.

Chapter 11 – Haneefah Muhammad

SURVIVING AND THRIVING

I decided 2020 would be my best year ever, my year
of saying YES!
YES to trying anything – new opportunities, new
experiences and new challenges.
Loads of things had happened in 2019, lots of
exciting experiences came my way
My first book of poems, my first women's retreat,
even a small part in a play!

So I was ready to step things up the moment we
entered this brand new year
There'd be no maybe's or perhaps's, I would push
through all my doubts and my fears.
And things started well – great family and friends,
Mum's health was good & so was mine
It was January I had a new sense of purpose, more
energy – these were exciting times.

I was following my inner voice along a deeper, soul-
based path
Guided by my intuition that was urging me to
remove the mask;
Facing my insecurities caused by the pain and hurt
from my past
Embracing my imperfections and honouring my real
self at last.

Life Inna Lockdown 2020

By February, I was writing more poems then
suddenly another play was looming.
I worked on my new website, was coaching, went to
meetings and I was also 'Zoom-ing'!
I started a new health plan, was getting fitter and my
work-out included swimming
I loved how I looked and how I felt, my confidence
was truly brimming.

By around mid-February there was stuff in the news
about people having 'flu-like symptoms
It mostly seemed they'd been abroad & brought the
sickness back with them.
I didn't give it much thought - I wasn't affected, so I
went on with my daily routines
Seeing my family, friends, went to the theatre a few
times just continued doing 'my thing'.

I kept my promise to say YES to trying new things and
life was getting better and better,
At times I was way out of my comfort zone - it was
scary, but I'm glad I put myself 'out there'.
The news reported more people getting sick with this
'flu but I still wasn't affected
I was enjoying my life and looking after myself so was
sure I'd be protected.

Haneefah Muhammad

February passed into March and life went on though
now there was talk of a major 'flu virus
Reports said hundreds were ill and people were
asking "I wonder if it will affect us?"
But like others I kept working on ideas for projects,
schemes and plans
I booked talks, presentations, performances but then
I heard about this place called Wuhan.

By mid March there was tension in the air, concern
about this deadly virus was increasing,
For the first time, I felt worried for my health and
wondered if I would become the next victim.
When the 'Coronavirus' pandemic came
handwashing was advised to reduce our risk of
infection
Wearing masks, gloves and keeping our distance
were measures introduced for our protection.

Bulk-buying food and household goods was rampant,
shop shelves were left empty
At times I went out shopping and was genuinely
scared someone would steal it from me!
Uncertainty and panic were setting in, fear and
confusion was gripping the nation.
With queues outside shops things like loo rolls and
cleaning products had to be rationed.

Life Inna Lockdown 2020

Schools, theatres, cinemas and workplaces were
closed and only essential travel was allowed
Planes grounded, religious services stopped and a
ban was placed on large gatherings or crowds.
There were strict limits on taking exercise – go to the
park or take a walk but only for one hour
That's when the meaning of 'social isolation' kicked
in, now I was truly 'INNA LOCKDOWN'.

So here I was stuck at home, swamped by stories
about where the virus came from
Claims, counter-claims, blame, shame, fake news,
half-truths - it just went on and on.
I struggled with being 'socially distanced' from
people I love but can't see or give a hug
And it's unnatural to be deprived of natural, human
contact because of this deadly bug.

I'm ok with being alone but I'm a people person, I
enjoy socialising and having fun
But I told myself "girl, it is what it is so do the best
that can be done:"
I took a deep breath and decided to look again at
how to handle being in lockdown
I could choose to be resentful or do something
meaningful just by turning it around.

Haneefah Muhammad

I thought of the times I used to say "there's not
enough hours in the day"
I couldn't go out and do the things I love but now I
had more time, so couldn't complain!
Luckily I'd been working from home anyway so was
used to organising my time,
I could use it creatively, do things I'd been putting off
or learn something new on line.

As time's gone by I've designed my own 'new
normal' way of being and doing
Once I decided to trust my instincts and take control
it was simply a matter of choosing -
I could go all 'drama queen' - wallow in sorrow, have
a virus crisis or a pandemic panic
Or I could step back, decide how I wanted my new
life to be, then go on and live it!

Ok it's not the same as going out but the good thing
is I'm at home and I'm safe
And for fresh air and exercise I can go in the garden,
no worries about the 2 metres space.
Going outside less gives me more time to go inside -
time for inner reflection
To re-evaluate my life, reconnect with my emotions
and re-imagine my future path and direction.

Life Inna Lockdown 2020

So it's the end of May 2020, summer's coming and
things are slowly on the move
Restrictions lifted on shops, schools re-opening and
now we can meet in small groups.
I'm glad I chose to see that being shut in didn't mean
that I was being shut down
I'm glad I chose to be positive - not just to survive
but to thrive 'INNA LOCKDOWN'.

About Haneefah Muhammad

Haneefah is a Soul Empowerment Coach and performance poet. She self-published her book **My Soul Purpose** in 2019 and describes it as a collection of her poems about life, living and learning, on her journey to self-discovery.

Haneefah has over twenty years of experience as a Social Worker, mainly working with people experiencing complex mental health issues. Her first book, **The A-Z of Stress Solutions,** includes practical tips to manage stress and for better health and wellbeing.

Family, friendships, spirituality and her African Caribbean cultural identity reflect the values that are important to Haneefah.

She has lived and worked in Bedfordshire for nearly twenty years and contributes to community groups in Luton including The Butterfly Project for women and the Bedfordshire & Luton Recovery College that focuses on mental wellbeing and recovery for adults.

Chapter 12 – Natrel Mystic

Birth of a New Me

I call this a transitioning period LOCKDOWN! What was my life like before?

J.O.B.S (Just Over Broke Survivor), trying to earn Steve Jobs' income, working all hours, all shifts, simply trying to make ends meet. Why? Well, let me tell ya! DEBT! Falling out of every orifice and tripping me up in every area of my life, affecting my relationships with family, friends, colleagues and basically anyone who seemed to be better off. I was so caught up in my quest to pay back the money I forgot to live. I was just surviving, barely.

Something had to change; it did, my health. I was diagnosed with a benign brain tumour which activated my prolactin gland back in 2012, but I knew something was wrong way before, probably from 1999. I was already suffering with severe depression from the huge amount of debt I had. How was I supposed to pay back the 30 thousand pounds I owed now that I was ill? At this stage, I had to look on the bright side and say at least it's not the original 100 thousand pounds I owed, and the tumour is not life-threatening; silver linings eh?

In 2010, I was unemployed as I had been dismissed from a very well-paid job after losing a horrible tribunal hearing. I had moved out of my home to shack up with someone, who I later found out did not really want to be with me, so I decided to declare bankruptcy. It seemed like the only choice I had. Apologies for being chronologically out of order but it's just to give you an idea of where my health and mind was during this time. The country is celebrating the Olympics, and I'm homeless, in debt and feeling like death.

Various J.O.B.S, I eventually ended up in the care industry. I needed a change of pace and was even willing to sacrifice my income; my health was more important than money, but only for a short while. The care industry needed more than I could give, and this led to another breakdown, a major one. Now, its 2018 and I'm sitting on the train track, yep, wanting to end it all. What was the point of going on, living THIS life, my life? Well, fortunately, the train didn't come as someone at the station before mine had beat me to it. Now what?

I started to use social media to escape my reality. I connected with a family member and they introduced me to a company that would help me start a legal side hustle. At first, I didn't see the benefits of the team I had joined, but I started to implement their advice and realised I had many skills that I had suppressed.

Life started to change, and despite my mental health struggles and still working long hours, I began to see changes in me and my life. I started to connect with people who reached out, so I reached back and then in 2019, I was housed, and my life started to have a little stability.

During 2018 I kept having visions, and I'd finally admitted to my family that I hated employment. You can imagine their faces. All this debt and again, no way to pay back what I owe, but I had a plan; part-time J.O.B.S with room to develop my own business.

Life Inna Lockdown 2020

2020 began with a plan and a list of goals; it's my time! In February, my new business Yard Foods is launched, and the feedback is amazing! I'm thinking I can do this! But then the Covid-19 2020 lockdown kicks in; there's no food in the shops; I haven't got money to bulk buy, NO! Not now! I'm just getting started.

Yard Food closes.

A few weeks in, I'm thinking this isn't so bad. I've been alone for eight years, so what's a few weeks? A piece a cake!

I'm a Key Worker now and my routine didn't change; I just got busier. As a carer, I had to wear gloves and the mask is great as I suffer from hay fever and it blocks out the pollen.

Then I saw this post "If you can't go outside, go within" so I did! Meditation to Yoga, reconnecting with family, my mum and brother especially, Zoom calls and Whatsapp groups, sewing, organising my home. The world had stopped, and I saw this an opportunity to take my foot off the pedal too. Being in my home in a town where I didn't know anyone apart from my brother and his family made me feel safe. Finally!

Lockdown has given me a chance to reconnect with nature. I've been standing on my balcony above the naked trees and day by day the leaves and flowers grow, and I can hear the birds again; what a beautiful moment, a real feeling of gratitude. From this moment, I've encouraged as many people as I could to see the chance we have had to do all the things we've been putting off.

I started sewing again. I haven't done that since secondary school. Then the organising started as I was moving from a one bedroom flat to a studio. It's not easy but I'm still grateful none the less and there staring at me from the corner of the room was my laptop. Six years of photos to sort through and file.

I have to be honest I've always had the time but never saw the reason and just put things off until whenever. But now, my mind-set has changed to mind-flow, and what I could see around me were my friends and family creating and enjoying newfound hobbies and I wanted that feeling too.

I focused and finally got serious about my life and my love of working on myself for myself and at the same time helping others.

It's Free Up not Lockdown!

My vocabulary has changed, and I have seen how speaking positivity into my life can manifest into a reality! The food business has been relaunched and the support and feedback are amazing.

I'd like to dedicate this piece of writing to my mum. Her resilience and strength has kept my mental health and sanity intact and to all the people who have checked up on me during this time, thank you. "Thank u 4 Tattie."

About Natrel Mystic

Natrel (aka) Ladybug is a daughter, granddaughter, sister, cousin and her favourite, an auntie.

Life and health prevented Natrel from birthing her own babies and at the time she thought this was a curse, but it has become the biggest blessing as she nurtures and mentors all children.

She has a vast array of hobbies and interests, from cooking to yoga. "I think I could cover A-Z with my list."

Natrel says, "My traumatic past is now my rocket fuel, so when they say the sky is the limit, I say NO, there are no limits in my future, and all I see are the Stars!"

Chapter 13 – Barbara Moses

...And Everything STOPPED

Before lockdown, life was a race; a race without a finish line and I was the star athlete who never seemed to get the trophy. With three boys, one husband, a full-time job as a teacher and a side hustle, it was truly non-stop.

My husband and I did it all. Cooking, cleaning, chauffeuring, attending church and all whilst trying to find time for myself to thrive. Just thinking about how it was before lockdown leaves me exhausted and I am determined not to be part of that race again as things return to normal.

During the lockdown I discovered something about myself that surprised and intrigued me. Before I get into that, I know there are those of us who might have been ill with the COVID-19 virus or lost loved ones due to the virus or even due to other reasons that the virus overshadowed. I want to say I'm truly sorry.

When I heard some of the tragic stories, my heart ached for the families and friends left behind. Husbands and wives that would never have their partners by their side to navigate this tricky world again; children that would not have their mum or dad to love, guide and guard them through life; and so much more.

A dear friend experienced a loss that shook me to the core and made me question my faith. In those moments of questioning and quiet reflection, I started writing and this is what I discovered about myself.

You see, as a teacher, I enjoy teaching pupils how to be great creative writers. I happen to be good at it (that is, the teaching of it), but strangely enough, I don't particularly enjoy writing myself, which is why I find it difficult to journal consistently. I do love to read, and I'm amazed at how some writers paint such beautiful pictures with words; how they mix and blend words together and serve such delicious stories, poems and information.

These are the first of my amateur musings and I want to dedicate them to all those who lost loved ones during this time with the hope that my words bring you some small comfort.

Be Still and Know

I will question God
I will ask him why
I will rage at him
I will ask him why
I will cry to him
I will ask him why
Then I will be still...
and know that you are God

A Peace That Passes Understanding

The pain of the loss of a child is a pain too deep to endure
A pain like no other, too much for any mother,
It is like slashing the heart into millions of pieces
With the sharpest of knives; an obsidian knife,
while still keeping the mother and father alive

But the Lord is close to the brokenhearted
He bestows strength beyond understanding,
A strength that only comes from above,
given to us by the Maker Himself,
who rescues those whose spirits are crushed,
and brings a peace that passes understanding.

Life Inna Lockdown 2020

During the COVID-19 Lockdown, I STOPPED! Imagine someone turning on a giant fan and everything is sent billowing up into the air, twirling and whirling then suddenly that fan is turned off. It was a beautiful stop! I could breathe again. I got to know my boys and my husband again, and more importantly, I got to know myself again. I created beautiful things with my hands and new ideas emerged from nowhere. I made the decision not to worry too much about the virus as that wasn't going to keep me or my family protected but rob me of joy. This was my new place; my happy place of taking things one step at a time, having time to think things through, becoming more creative and inspired until the world went mad again.

I woke up one morning to the horror of watching another man snuff the life of a black man despite his pleas of "I can't breathe", and I too couldn't breathe. That image assaulted my sensibilities and is forever seared in mind. I made the decision not to be silent, and once again, I wrote.

What is it a about the colour of my skin that irks you?

Is this about me or is this really about you?

Where do the bitter waters of hate flow from?

Are you threatened by the rich amber of my complexion?

Is it the honey-like smoothness of my skin that galls you?

Or the sumptuous fullness of my lips that vexes you?

Is it the well-rounded firmness of my buttocks that rattles you?

What is it a about the colour of my skin that irks you?

Is this about me or is this really about you?

Where do the bitter waters of hate flow from?

Is it my wide hips that dances to the rhythm of mother earth

That annoys you?

Are you intimidated by the richness of my heritage,

the strength of my spirit and my refusal to cower?

Is it my quiet endurance and strength of forbearance?

even in the face of your abhorrence that terrifies you?

WHAT IS IT ABOUT MY BLACK BEAUTY THAT THREATENS YOU?

Despite the tragedy of this lockdown, it came with some unexpected blessings. I am full of emotions, a mix of feelings that I am still sorting through. I am grateful, sad, angry, confused, excited, afraid, inspired, hopeful, determined, encouraged and so on. But one thing I am most hopeful about is that there is hope for humanity and that I have a part to play and that I never want to go back to the race that I let life put me in. I need to find my own race; one that isn't a sprint but a marathon, for as the Holy Book says:

...the race is not to the swift nor the battle to the strong...
...but time and chance happen to us all.
Ecclesiastes 9:11

About Beulah (aka Barbara)

Beulah is a mother, wife, teacher, crafter and much more. Before becoming a teacher, she was a lawyer. Why the switch? "Hmmm… that is a story for another time."

Beulah loves creating with her hands and has fallen in love with the art of paper floristry. "It's a beautiful art form which I absolutely love."

Beulah is also an amateur Cross-Fitter. "I love the workouts and have discovered a lot about myself doing Cross Fit."

She took part in writing for this book as she believes it will inspire, entertain, educate and give hope to many. Beulah felt that this was definitely something worth being a part of.

Chapter 14 – Munyaradzi Sajanga

Days of Reacon

Since the 23 March 2020, the United Kingdom has been on lockdown to help stop the spread of the Covid-19 virus. Now, weeks later we are still in lockdown and no one knows when this is going to end.

The path to happiness begins and ends in your mind, so it was time to free my mind and my life to follow. I realised that all we control in life is how we respond to life.

We have always been busy, and now we have been made to slow down. In other words, for me, it's like I have been shut down and then set to restart mode.

The universe has given us this situation as if to say...

"We need to find ways to slow down, so life does not rush right past us. We need to start noticing more beauty to lift our spirits and keep us inspired. We need to give ourselves permission to let go of judgement and the endless pursuit of perfection. And we need to start seeing each other, and ourselves, for the perfectly imperfect treasures that we are."

I love this quote from my mentor Beth

"Letting go of what you think should be, does not mean giving up on what could be."

This situation has also brought in opportunities for rethinking our priorities and perspective. A few months ago, I was so focused on my upcoming Africa Music Festival scheduled for the 18 July 2020 and now my focus is ensuring my family are in a good head space during this time and trying to keep my business going whilst working from home.

My focus in life is now shifted and I am more grateful to life and what I have than ever before. I took everything for granted and as they say it's not until you lose something that you realise it's worth.

My intention every day is about contribution. When you move your focus from 'me' to 'we', you enable yourself to be energised by a larger cause greater than yourself. Every day is different. Some days are good, and some are not. On the days, I feel like I have achieved nothing, I learned that by simply picking up the phone and checking in on someone else to lift their day is equally a win.

I learned to give my loved one's space to express themselves and explore their emotions. Anger, frustration, sadness, anxiety and a feeling of being overwhelmed are just some of the emotions that naturally arise. It's not easy to be able to help them shift to a more beneficial place like gratitude. We have a daily ritual where everyone can share what the best part of the day was and at least one thing they are grateful for. So far this has been working well for us.

It is still not certain when everything will be back to normal, or shall I say when we can start over again. I'm more concerned about surviving and with the rest, I can figure it out when the time comes. Right now, I'm focusing on my family's health and happiness.

About Munyaradzi Sajanga aka Lady Munya

Munyaradzi was born in Zimbabwe in 1976 and has been residing in the UK since 2002.

She is a mother and a passionate businesswoman. She loves music and watching the TV. Munya also enjoys organising and hosting community events and programmes.

Chapter 15 – Patricia Isaie

Challenging Change

"Oh Boris, when are you going to close the schools?" These were the words that were rippling through my school and the wider community. Classroom pupil numbers had already begun to dwindle from the beginning of the week. Then came those words, "Schools will be closing in the UK on 20 March!"

That week school became a hive of activity as we prepared our pupils for their unknown descent into home-learning, packing them away with home activities, stationery, and words of cheer and wisdom. They expected us to have all the answers, "What's happening Miss when are we coming back?" That Friday, 20 March, at home time as we said our goodbyes, it felt like we were waving war evacuees to unknown uncertainty.

Life Inna Lockdown 2020

Roll on one week later! It was my birthday; it was a Friday, and the sun was shining, the weather was hot, I was home alone, my husband was at work and my son was at his daycare facility. At the beginning of the year, I had been overly excited that my birthday was at the end of the working week.

I was at least going to go out for a meal for my birthday, but all the restaurants were now closed. Staying in was now the new going out!

Ah well, I would settle for baking my own Victoria Sandwich birthday cake; simple but satisfying and I would celebrate with my husband and son. Incidentally, it turned out good. Lockdown birthday cake with a few little trimmings went down well.

The new dreaded 'C' word was Coronavirus. Those of my age group associated corona with a fizzy drink of the 1970's. Strange name I thought. I listened as much as I could to the 'Do's and Don'ts'. The television seemed to be permanently set to the BBC News as I waited each day for the 'latest update.'

The second week of lockdown was really 'lockdown.' I had company at home now as my son's daycare facility (he has autism and learning difficulties) was now officially closed. I was worried because I would have to keep him entertained from Monday to Friday but relieved at the same time that he was safely at home and protected from this terrible, potentially killer virus! Anyone who has any links with autism will know that it can present many challenges. I took a deep breath and muttered under my breath "Right, you can do this, Patricia, one, two, three..."

My living room became the new Autism Centre; gathering everything that would relieve the hours and days, i.e. meditation CDs, games and puzzles. My Blue Peter skills came back to me as I created a home-made bowling game that consisted of spraying four water bottles in silver, a yoga mat and a small plastic ball! Simple things! That's all it took. Who cares that my living room looked a little chock-a-block and chaotic? Nobody was going to be coming around anyway now that households were not permitted to mix. Together with having nature's good weather and being able to go out into the garden, I think I coped fairly well and had complete admiration and respect for my son's support workers more so than I ever did!

I wondered to myself, what was going through my son's mind? Autism is complex enough, and now his world had completely changed. What was he thinking, where were his familiar surroundings? Things were completely different for him at home compared to his usual daycare surroundings. No trampoline in the garden. No countryside scenery. Thanks to the grace of God, we were still able to access weekend respite care, but at first, it was a case of "should I, or shouldn't I?"

Those weekend respite days away from home were beneficial as I could see the happiness and spring in his step on arrival back at home. And what about me? Who cares for the carer? Giving my son regular respite breaks gave me a short time period to re-charge my batteries and reclaim some 'me time.'

On the sixth week of lockdown, I went back to work as a teaching assistant to support keyworker children and vulnerable children with a few of my work colleagues. The day was filled with fun activities for the small handful of children that had ventured out to school. The numbers were quite low in comparison to how many we were expecting but stepping out that day did me the world of good and was just the tonic I needed.

I have only touched on a small part of lockdown and so many emotions, feelings and thoughts have passed through that middle-aged brain of mine. It's been a time of catching up, trying new things and participating in some of my hobbies. I love sewing, taking walks, and getting to grips with the new ways of communicating, i.e. Whatsapp and Zoom.

It's been a case of survival even on the smallest of levels. Toothache decided to test me during lockdown, with a chipped filling, hot and cold sensitivity and throbbing pain! What more could I wish for when there weren't any dentists open? I discovered from a friend how beneficial clove oil was for toothache and with the power of prayer my pain disappeared. I will still be in that queue when the dentists do open that's for sure.

The future…I don't know. I have changed, I've got to have changed and my job has changed. The world has changed. I now value life in a way that I never did before. Fresh air, being in the garden, being able to speak to friends and family remotely. A big family meet-up is guaranteed with big hugs for everyone when this is over.

As I write this, I think to myself who would have known what was around the corner at the start of the year. This virus started in China, then leap-frogged over to Europe but still we thought we were safe. We were then gripped with fear, confusion, chaos, panic and loss of lives in the thousands. All I can say is "World, please get well soon, from me to you."

About Patricia Isaie

Patricia is British born of Jamaican parentage and married with two wonderful children.

She works as a teaching assistant in a school and gets an immense amount of satisfaction working with children.

This is the first time she has contributed to a book and Patricia is extremely grateful and proud to have been asked.

She is a self-confessed 'creative type' and enjoys sewing and frequently exhibits at community events. Her other passions are reading, cooking, travelling and meeting with people.

Chapter 16 – Helen Garrand

From Caterpillar to Butterfly

Before this COVID-19 virus arrived, my life revolved around being a charity shop volunteer, going shopping, meeting up with friends and running a weekly coffee morning. When I wasn't doing this, I would be at home meeting with my partner and doing housework and knitting. I would swim once a week, and this is how my life went on. Very similar to the way that a caterpillar searches for food in the same mundane way that it takes for granted.

With the caterpillar, the time comes in its life when it has to form a cocoon around itself. Our cocoon was the lockdown. I am now alone in my house and told I can't go out when I want to. I feel low and that nobody cares. I wonder what I can do or whether I can be bothered to do it. I speak to friends and family on the phone but not in person. People are dying and in hospital, and I am frightened to go out even though I can have an hour's exercise. Things are changing. I am changing but have no control over it just as the caterpillar has no control of the changes that are occurring whilst it is in the cocoon.

How can I manage the change? How can I take control? I will walk to see the horses and meet new friends on Zoom. I will start to learn new skills; maybe become the gardener I have never been. I will knit hearts for the loved ones and do computer courses. The list is endless. I am developing and changing, and I must keep positive.

And so, little by little, the caterpillar starts to emerge from the cocoon, only it is no longer a mundane caterpillar but a glorious butterfly. And so, the lock down begins to ease. I can again go to the shops, but it is different. You can't go in immediately now and you must queue which makes you think how we used to take this for granted. I am emerging from my cocoon with a fantastic garden which I have been able to tender despite my disability. I am learning and developing my skills. Life in the cocoon of lockdown has shown me that there is light on the other side. A light which is unique to each and every one of us.

As the butterfly prepares to find its wings to fly, so too do we. We can use the experience and the skills we have gained to go forward and work out what it is we want to achieve (our wings). My wings will be to continue the garden and be able to enjoy looking at my handiwork thinking "Wow!"

I will return to my charity work, but it will be different. Making new friends on Zoom has also taught me I need to get out there and seize every opportunity to make friends as we all need each other.

About Helen Garrand

Helen has a nursing background but hasn't practiced since 2005. Having moved to Leeds in 1994 to gain her BA (Honours) degree in Psychology and Sociology, Helen ended up staying there and became a 'Northern lass.'

Since not being able to work due to a disability, Helen has in the past organised music festivals, carnivals and presently organises the annual Christmas Lights switch-on event in the area where she lives.

She also undertakes volunteer work at the local PDSA Shop and is very privileged to have been awarded the title Retail Volunteer of the Year 2018 for the whole of the PDSA. Helen was also shortlisted down to the last five in the National Third Sector Excellence Awards in 2019.

Chapter 17 – Cecile Terrelonge

Vita

It's a few weeks to April 2020, and I have been working really hard splitting myself between two jobs, so I am really looking forward to the two music gigs I have coming up. Live music fills my soul with happiness and enjoyment. Something else that fills my soul with happiness is family and spending time with them. Easter is on its way and with that brings the usual cook up of fish, drinks, and family. I can't wait! I keep hearing about the Coronavirus and how it is affecting other countries, especially China, but I am sure we will be fine. It is far away enough to not affect us. It will be fine; Good Friday, cook up, Easter Sunday gig; life is good!

Things are starting to get a little scary as everyone is talking about the Coronavirus and PPE (personal protective equipment) or the lack of it. I have a lot of family members who work in the NHS, or Social Care, including myself and I am concerned how this is going to affect us all. On our family WhatsApp group, we are looking to support those of us that may now be furloughed or even unemployed due to the changes that are coming into effect. But it will be OK. I am sure it will.

Now it is really starting to feel real. I just received a message to say that my cousin is in hospital with Coronavirus symptoms and she is very poorly. NO VISITORS ALLOWED! Both of my children work at the hospital she is in. Surely as staff they could visit. She is my son's Godmother. Can he see her? NO VISITORS ALLOWED. Now I am really scared.

We are now in lockdown. The shops are shut. The roads are clear, and a lot of people are at home because they have been told to stay at home. Some are working from home; some have been furloughed and some have lost their jobs. I am still going to work and driving around feels really eery. It feels like Christmas Day when the roads are empty, but now it is because there is a deadly virus in Britain and the government are trying to protect everyone by getting them to stay at home. I support clients in the community who are elderly, vulnerable, and may have a learning disability or mental health issue. They need us for many different reasons, but they do need us and that is why I am still going to work.

The food shops are open so that everyone can do their weekly shopping, but this can be a nightmare. Some of the shops have set up specific times for the elderly and vulnerable and for the NHS and social care staff. In some shops, the NHS staff and social care staff can go to the front of the queue, but I feel really guilty when I go to the front of the queue. I feel sorry for those who are having to queue. What is annoying is customers who do not stick to the one-way system in the supermarkets or don't keep two metres away from me, as this is the Government guidelines. My daughter gets really stressed by this, and I can see her anxiety levels rise, so we are limiting our shopping to a minimum.

My cousin has now come out of the hospital and she is recuperating at home. She is not out of the woods yet, but she is home with her family looking after her, so that is good. What is not good is the number of infected people, and the death rate is increasing by the day. At our local hospital, where my children work, there is a ward set aside for patients with the virus and although I know they do not work anywhere near that ward, it makes me nervous that they are working there. They tell me they are OK, but I am not sure because I tell them that I am alright, and I don't know if that is true. We have some PPE, gloves and aprons but we have run out of hand sanitiser. The company I work for have not been able to find any online and the shops do not have any. We have a few masks but not a lot. I know they tell us that washing our hands frequently with soap and water is fine, but I would feel a little better with some hand sanitiser. I am very near to finishing the one I had at home, that concerns me. I have also come to the end of my packet of paracetamol tablets because the shops have also sold out of them. I take these for the pain I have from Fibromyalgia, and I try not to take them every day, but some days I really need them and ultimately, to be able to work, I have family and friends on the lookout for me. Hoorah! Superdrug and Boots now have hand sanitiser and paracetamol.

And what about Zoom? Wow! This is a positive aspect that has come out of lockdown. I am not very good with technology, but I have mastered Zoom and I can talk to my family, friends and clients via Zoom. I am also part of another community where we have a weekly Thursday Zoom session, and we talk about many different things, share lots of information that can be helpful to many and, we support each other. This has been very important to me during this difficult time.

Looking to the future, I am hoping with all my might that my family, whether close or extended, come out of this in one piece. From tomorrow the country will start the process of coming out of lockdown. This really scares me, and I do not know how this will look but I can do this. Lockdown has increased my enthusiasm to change my working life so that counselling will be my main role and social care will become my second role. I can also see writing in my future so there are scary but exciting times ahead!

About Cecile Terrelonge

Cecile has two fabulous children and has been a Registered Manager in the social care sector for over 26 years. She supports adults with learning disabilities, mental health issues and the elderly in the community.

Cecile has also been a counsellor for 16 years, working with adults, youths, and children. She runs a voluntary counselling service for young people from the ages of 11 years to 25 years.

Although she will be continuing to work within the social care field, Cecile will be doing more work as a counsellor and a life coach, working within the community.

This is her first piece of writing, but she feels it is the first of many. "Exciting times ahead."

Chapter 18 – Remie Dominique

The Turning Tides

Life is organised chaos for me right now. There are so many different things that are happening to me and around me at the minute that are both good and bad, but that's life. I'm always grateful for everything that happens to me in life as it becomes a lesson no matter what, but at the moment, it can be very hectic on the mind.

I have recently started to get back to my normal self after a big life change, which left me in quite a dark place. And once in a dark place, silly decisions can be made. I decided to stop taking anti-depressants without consulting my doctor or family as I wanted to ride the pain out. I knew it would be hard, but I wanted to have the satisfaction of knowing I could overcome my low moods, a naive assumption. At the time, it was rough and allowing myself to be alone with my thoughts all over again was extremely hard. I realised I had to start taking my medication again, pretty quickly into my little 'experiment' but the Coronavirus situation had started to take over all our lives.

Because I work at a hospital, I have had quite an insider view to the COVID-19 virus from the beginning, but I, like so many others, haven't had any real understanding of quite how intense and scary this would become and how it would affect us day-to-day. Because of this, I did not bat an eyelid. I carried on as normal.

But I could not have been more wrong. As everything was slowing down and we started to go into lockdown, I realised quite early on that I was struggling to get the medication I needed to help myself through this, which is very scary. I pushed my hardest to get my anti-depressants and was successful after many tries, but it left me in doubt of how many others would be able to get hold of important medications.

As each work shift went by, the hospital became much more regimented and on edge, preparing themselves for what was to come. Procedures were being put in place and I was breaking down. At home, my brother had just moved back in as we were unsure whether he would be able to secure his new house with everything that was going on.

During the time that I had stopped taking anti-depressants, my body reacted to the 'cold turkey' method at first and I honestly felt like I was dying. But I felt I couldn't tell anybody except my mum. I was not myself. I felt nauseated, dizzy, and I felt like I was on drugs, but I just had to wait for this to subside.

And subside it did. Straight into full lockdown.

Boris Johnson, the Prime Minister, had spoken and we were to quarantine. My depression had subsided, and my mood felt back on track. Plus, my anxiety had begun to settle. I was finally able to start using my photography and videography skills again and to create Safety videos for the Hospital Trusts which was an amazing achievement. I am proud of myself... I think...

However, I feel bad. I feel bad knowing that so many people have lost their jobs, but I am still able to go to work every day. I feel bad knowing that there are families across the world who have been split up, yet (although not my entire family), I am isolating with mine and am able to see them every day. I feel bad that nobody is being given the full story by the media. Working in the hospital, I had never expected to see the things I had seen so early on. I want to do more; I want to be able to help more.

I have had varying degrees of thought throughout lockdown about the dreaded work selfishness. Am I being selfish for wanting and needing a break from work while others can't work? Am I selfish for using my NHS card at the supermarket? Am I selfish for enjoying not having to go to social events with lots of people? And I've decided NO. Whilst in lockdown, I have realised that the organised chaos I was enduring before lockdown doesn't have to be forever. But the life I am living whilst in lockdown will also not be forever.

Bundled up anxieties I didn't even realise I had, surfaced during the lockdown and I'm not scared anymore because lockdown has taught me to be free. Life will carry on no matter what circumstances we are in, no matter who we are able to see. So why am I stressing over the little things? I am taking the time to make the most of the things I enjoy because I will never be given this time again. My visions, much like before lockdown, have mostly stayed the same. I want to be successful in my chosen career; I want to support my family and help them be the best they can be. But my visions are much clearer now.

I don't have to feel a burden or scared by the path that is being laid out for my future. I just need to take the time to figure it out. I don't know when lockdown will be completely over or when we will return to 'normal', but I do know that we are all still living. We may be living a 'new normal' but we are still living, and I am grateful for this. I am grateful and excited to see what our new normal brings my way.

About Remie Dominique

Remie is a 22-year-old photographer/videographer who loves to spread some happiness and strength into the world. She is a strong believer in taking everything that happens to her and turning it into a lesson that she can learn from.

Whilst at university, Remie became a survivor of domestic abuse and she chooses to help other people from her experience rather than allowing it to consume her. She decided to make a documentary about her story and shows others how to get the help they need.

Remie is also a mental health advocate and wants to help people find a safe place within themselves so they can be the best person they can be!

Chapter 19 – Letitia Lorraine Thomas

My Journey to Uncertainty

Well, like everybody else, lockdown hasn't been easy for me. I am trying to keep myself busy and happy watching documentaries and films on Netflix, doing pieces of work for the Disability Resource Centre. I have been talking to my family and friends and checking all is OK.

I don't watch the news often because I find it negative and confusing as it makes me question; do they know what we are dealing with, or are they just guessing? I have heard lots of different information about the current situation and how it came about but I really don't know what to believe at the moment.

I think that the new guidelines that the government have put in place are the same, but they have worded it differently. We need more information on what they're doing to find a cure and how many people are surviving the virus as this negative press is not doing anyone any good mentally.

I have been thinking about my own mental health since being in lockdown more than I would normally, and I have to say that we all have to look after our own mental health no matter what we are doing in our lives.

Sometimes we need to have a day or an hour to clear our minds, shut out the negative thoughts and people. This has been really helping me and I will continue with this practice after lockdown.

I have been supporting my best friend through some tough days. We have been talking about the good old days when we used to hang out with each other, and other girls were so jealous of our friendship because they wanted his attention, but I got all of his attention.

We need more TV programmes about mental health and less about the virus because when this is over people are going to require counselling or other support services to deal with their mental health.

I know that people with depression and anxiety who are being told to stay in are finding it difficult and I know from staying in myself it does make you want to go out and socialise even though we are not allowed to. But we are not alone, we just socialise virtually now.

I think it's great that we can video call and have group meetings on our smart devices, but I do feel sorry for people who do not have access to this type of technology.

The garden has become my outdoor saviour as I am not allowed to go anywhere else. My neighbour is a blessing as he has been cutting my grass for me.

Some days I think why I am getting up and dressed because there is nowhere to go and nobody can come and chill with me, but then again, everybody's going through the same thing.

I have noticed that If I don't check in on my best friend or talk to any of my friends, I don't feel good. My best friend always asks how I am mentally because he knows that I like to go out and engage in different activities.

I am honest with my bestie some days; however, I have days where I really struggle but talking with friends or blasting my music always helps.

What a blow! I was really looking forward to this weekend because Friday was going to be the Luton Carnival and I was going to be the Carnival Queen, but due to the virus, it has been cancelled. I also had to postpone my post-birthday celebrations on Saturday night, so my dad is going to treat me to a takeaway and a bottle of wine.

Well, I certainly had a 34th birthday to remember as it was definitely different, but I must say I am truly blessed and grateful to have such amazing family and friends in my life that made my lockdown birthday very special.

I cannot wait until this is all over when I can meet up with my family and friends for a really good celebration and I can get back to my workout routine. I never thought I would miss my workout, but I actually do.

I have been speaking to my personal trainer and I have decided that I am going to start working out again. However, before I made the decision, I had a conversation with my mum about it, and she said it was my decision, so it was confirmed, and I would start my work out again the following Wednesday.

I think that not being able to do whatever I want has made me realise how important family and friends are and how I want to have my own radio show or be in a TV show, and get back on the dating scene. I'm not sure if dating sites are the best way to meet a new partner, but I will try anything once or twice because I'm not giving up on love.

I am grateful that my Aunty Dee gets me involved in all different events as I have met inspirational people and have been given great opportunities.

We are all helping the NHS by staying in. I just want to say a big thank you to the NHS and the carers who are doing their jobs every day and I really appreciate all of you.

I think that we should have a national NHS and carers day after this.

Till the next time keep following your dreams and stay blessed and safe!

About Letitia Lorraine Thomas

Letitia, also known as Tishy, is 34 years old and was born with a disability called Cerebral Palsy which affects the brain and different parts of the body. For Tishy, this affects her speech, her arms and her legs so she uses a wheelchair to get around.

Tishy has a very supportive mum and dad, and a younger sister who is one of her best friends. She lives independently in the community in her own bungalow and is supported by carers and her family.

She is a volunteer at the Disability Resource Centre in Dunstable and the Pamtengo Radio Station where she assists with their social media production and campaigns.

Tishy is the Creative Director for Veronica Ebanks and is part of the promotions team for Simply Deez events...

Tishy doesn't let anything or anyone stop her from doing what she wants because, "I am a human being just like everybody else."

Chapter 20 – Pamela E Thompson

Lockdown – Unlocked Emotions

Lockdown may be a drain and driving me insane, but
now it's time to go inside to unravel the feelings I
could no longer hide
I asked my heart to let me in, to unlock the darkness
held deep down within I had to stop battling with
myself, I was hurting me and nobody else.

Those feelings that I feel, it's time to observe them
and keep it real, it's time to be honest with myself as
I now become the explorer and observer of self.

Time to journey deep within to unlock the beauty
that lies within, the true meaning of me, it's time to
set my spirit free and release negative energy.

Life Inna Lockdown 2020

The negativity in my mind that had built up overtime,
was driving me insane and hurting my poor brain,
trying to think outside the box of this mind of
negative knots, I just wanted to run and hide from all
this raw emotion running wild inside

I felt like the world owed me for keeping me in
captivity, not giving me a way out so in my mind I
would scream and shout. Heads rolling night and day
because the demons don't go away, I felt the need to
lash out to get this trauma out

Lockdown had me beat, but I would not allow it to
defeat, the strong person that I am, so it was time to
make a stand. I found another way and began to
meditate with my guardian angel day by day, I found
something that worked for me to raise my vibration
and my energy

I have passed the test of endurance, I am here to tell
the tale, now it's time to sit back, relax, as I can
finally exhale
This journey has been long and arduous, on that we
can all agree, but there is nothing better than peace
of mind and a newfound love for me

The pain in my head is there no more as I finally
found the key, and unlocked the door to the negative
thoughts in my mind and replaced them with
thoughts that were loving and kind
That anger in my brain no longer drives me insane.
No more pulling of my hair because now I
actually care

No more judgements passed by me as everyone has
a choice in this life of who they want to be, let's
choose to live and let live, and choose peace and
harmony

Lockdown was no longer a drain and was no longer
driving me insane, a failure I am not, because I don't
feel good all the time, I am a hero because I kept
going that extra mile, so to ensure that every day I
awake with a loving smile

About Pamela E Thompson

Pamela began writing poetry two years ago after losing her Auntie to Cancer. She found that writing about her raw emotions gave her a sense of release that she had never felt before. The more she wrote, the more she began to heal from past traumatic experiences and the loss she was feeling.

Developing an understanding and awareness of her own fears and prejudices has enabled Pamela to develop personally. She has a passion to empower and inspire others to gain a deep understanding of self through her words of expression.

Being part of this book collaboration has enabled her to step outside of her comfort zone and she is truly grateful to be part of this wonderful experience.

134

Chapter 21 – Jo Maddix

Self-Care

I wake up early in the morning and go for a run. I drive to town and meet my sister for lunch and chat about the latest news about a virus in Wuhan, China, that is transferred from bats which the Chinese people eat as a delicacy. We take a stroll through the shops before I leave to pick up my daughter from work. I pop into the grocery store and buy something nice for dinner. That was the week before the world changed and everyone was confined to their homes, only leaving for necessary groceries, one hour of exercise and jobs considered as key working.

It's the middle of March 2020. I look into the mirror and wonder when the grey of my hennaed roots, tinted eyebrows and eyelashes will resurface like the conspirators of fake news blowing up my phone, telling me the cause of COVID-19 is the radiation from 5G waves on smartphones. No, it's the Second Coming. It's a government conspiracy to kill the black and poor people by lethal injection. Don't take the vaccine, it has a chip designed to track your every move. You catch the virus through your eyes; you get it through breathing; it came from Wuhan in China. No, it came from Australia on a plane. No, it's man-made. At the mercy of fake news,

I search social media looking for news of a cure.
I watch the news, listen to the radio and soak up all the information about Coronavirus, passing on news from so-called experts. I am frightened for me, for my parents, for my children, for my family, I'm losing trust in establishments, losing hope when Coronavirus affects the country's Prime Minister and worried about the political unrest when people break the rules of lockdown.

I count the wrinkles on my forehead and count one, two, three; the exact number of weeks I have been in lockdown except it feels like an age.

I look into my eyes and search for the expression of sympathy, empathy, some connection to the hundreds and thousands of people reported about in the daily news to have succumbed to the virus. Do my eyes fill with tears of pain for the children I have not parented, the brother or sister I never had, and mother or father I never knew. My expression changes with a thought which brings a light in my eyes of recognition and the familiar, as I wonder whether I have enough toilet paper and food for the next six months.

I close my eyes and thoughts of hospital beds full of people on ventilators unable to breathe on their own, the stealth of COVID-19 visiting all, irrespective of age, class or race.

I envisage empty graves waiting for the people unable to say goodbye, reminisce, hold hands, give a hug, shed a parting tear, feel the warmth leaving the body as they leave to a place of no return, no celebration of the life they had, no washing of the dead and preparing for burial. I step into the bath and immerse myself into sweet water smelling of forget-me-nots, touching the fat of my stomach, wondering how I can make it disappear forever.

I listen to the news of lockdown, isolation, domestic violence on the increase, poor mental health, antibacterial sprays, queues, social distancing, all over the world. I look at my hands and prepare them for service, washing the palms, back, sides, fingers, thumbs, adorn my personal protective equipment, gloves, apron and mask, and I promise not to touch my face. I receive news of some friends and acquaintances who have died after contracting COVID-19 related illnesses due to underlying health problems. I speak to friends who are experiencing symptoms but have not been tested.

I selfishly worry about losing them and think about the families left behind by their loved ones, wondering how they will pick up the pieces and move on with their lives.

I open my mouth and hear myself giving counsel and comfort, trying to find the words and shape them into messages that bring solace and chicken soup for the soul, buying groceries for the high risk, giving financial assistance, arranging a bed for the sick, asking myself how long has it been since I spoke to certain friends, pondering on the shortness of life. Feeling tired, drained, emotionally and mentally, I apply lip balm to my chapped lips and drink green juice to sustain my body.

The world is a different place: no restaurants, shops, theatres, cinemas and parks, no children playing on the streets. I listen and hear nothing, my heart beats to a timeless drum, sleep eludes me, and my chest falls and rises to the peak of the pandemic. Death rates start to fall. Slowly, the world attempts to get back to a new normal. People wanting answers, politicians asking for enquiries, was the country too slow at getting on top of the pandemic? Why are certain groups more prone to the virus?

I stop reading fake news and switch off my mobile phone. I feel the rhythm of life pulsing through my veins and slowing down to an easy pace, in step with my walk. I say "Good Morning" to anyone I see. The sunshine touches my body, and the breeze tickles my face. I feel a sense of peace and happiness and light.

I am listening to nature and seeing the world in colour. My mind is clear, and I have no worries. It's quiet, no sound of moving vehicles, road rage, chaos, noise, pressure.

I breathe clean air.

I look in the mirror and know my roots, eyebrows and eye lashes are grey. My face is smooth, and my eyes are clear. My body feels healthy and strong. I am working from home, not driving, spending more time with my family. I am more organised, life is no longer hectic, and I am not going out all the time. It feels better; the world is healing. I don't want to go back. From now on, I will put myself first and pay attention to self-care.

About Jo Maddix

Jo is from London and has a background in mental health and social work. In her spare time, Jo is involved in voluntary work for a charitable organisation, she oversees their social media and young person's group.

Her hobbies include travelling, running, and reading and she would like to try her hand at writing a book one day.

Chapter 22 - Dee Bailey

Rise Up – You Got This!

A week before Christmas and I am now working from home. I would say to friends, "I'm on lockdown!" It was stressful and I did feel the pressure, worrying whether I would still have a job. During this period, my husband was away, so some days I did not cook, some days I did not shower. Why should I? It was only me and I could not be bothered. I found it very easy to log on to my computer, and when I brought my head up, I found myself still in my dressing gown, and it was after 5pm!

I was officially made redundant at the end of January 2020 and then found a new job starting mid-February. The relief, I cannot explain, after nearly two months of being at home. Whoopee, Hallelujah!

Life Inna Lockdown 2020

No longer at home all day, I was super excited, so I went out and purchased a whole new wardrobe for my new job in the office. Currently feeling blessed, new job, new clothes, the family is good, holiday coming... Life was really good!

Simply Deez Events International Women's Day celebration went well on 7 March 2020. The numbers for the event were much lower than the previous year but we still raised £1,000 for the Alzheimer's Society. Rumbles of the COVID-19 virus were getting louder. The 21 March could not come soon enough; the countdown is on; I am in holiday mode. Montserrat (a small island in the Caribbean) Rum Punch, mangoes, guava jelly, fresh fish and of course my family are waiting for me. My nieces are sending me fabulous pictures, videos and Skyping every day. I'm jealous.

You know when you have that gut feeling? I am studying the news and checking the airlines every minute to see what the updates are; not good. I had to make the decision on 19 March not to travel as per Foreign Office guidelines and stayed here in the UK. My mother who was in Montserrat had to fly back early, due to the closure of airports, with my sister and my nieces.

Things are starting to move really fast; people are scared, many people are now being told to work from home. The UK is on lockdown. No way! I have been back in an office for approximately one month, and now I'm having to work from home AGAIN. Noooo! This is not what I wanted to hear. So many people want to work from home; families are spending more time together, and all the other positives.

Yes, I was being selfish, is that wrong of me? So, I filled up my petrol tank for the first time in years, went to the shops and started to stock up. The 'New' Lockdown had begun for me.

I usually organise physical events and I had an idea to bring people together where we could share our experiences and support one another online. An online event. Life was changing so rapidly for all of us so a weekly meeting it is! This is where #lifeinnalockdown2020 began.

At home every day, the dining room has now doubled up and is my office. Stuck in front of the computer for eight hours, I could feel my waistline and backside expanding. Laptop on, Breakfast TV on in the background, I would be watching the news all day long. Five o'clock would be the Prime Minister's briefing and then the news would continue throughout the day. I was overloaded with the news; no escape from this virus situation as it was also advertised on social media too. "Enough!" I decided, for my own mental wellbeing, no more TV during the day and no more watching the news or scrolling through social media with regards to the virus.

I'm forever grateful to my brother who purchased a smartphone for my mum as she can now video call us on WhatsApp! She is currently shielding and between us, my siblings and I, do the shopping and pick up prescriptions, etc... and help within the social distancing guidelines. It is hard to see her knowing her independence has been taken away. I do see my mum, but not being able to hug and squeeze her is not the same. I have not seen my grandchildren and I'm missing them badly.

We have Skype calls and the youngest who is two runs away from the screen. She says "No, Nanna." Ha, ha, wait till I catch her! She's forgotten Nanna run tings!

As the weeks go on this rumble is getting louder. Special hospitals are being built, thousands of people are dying and infected, Thursday evening is for clapping for the NHS, #lifeinnalockdown Zoom, no toilet paper (seriously), no pasta, or flour, the shelves are empty, no traffic jams, no flights, no buses or trains, there are hardly any passengers. The hairdressers, non-essential shops and schools are closed. Yet, people are smiling more, and the sun is shining; things are not that bad. This lockdown is different. I had to adjust my mindset and the way I do things. It's called survival.

My husband has just stepped in and shakes his head. He takes a quick look at the screen and walks off. Yes, I am on another #lifeinnalockdown Zoom!

I am listening to my body more and being kinder to me. There is a time to be still. Grrr, the weight is piling on. I do try and get out for a walk for three to four days a week in the park. The new work wardrobe no longer fits, and we are now in Summer!

So, I will continue walking, continue to try and eat healthier, give thanks, take each day at a time and when allowed, spend more time with family and friends and continue supporting the village the way I know how. I am being me, feeling blessed and doing what makes me happy!

Life Inna Lockdown 2020

Snapshot of my thoughts; Saturday 30 May 2020 16.49

Black people are more likely to die from the virus?

George Floyd is dead
#BlackLivesMatter

Dry your tears girl, why you crying?

The pain is there, it has always been there, just heightened now

Got to keep reminding myself this is 2020
Life does not stand still
Until we meet again.

About Dee Bailey

Dee is a wife, mother, grandmother, daughter, sister, friend. "This is what they put on your headstone!"

"Yes, I am all of the above but most of all I am me!"

Dee loves her family and friends and is also very passionate about the community and village where she lives, especially the young people and making a difference in her own way. For over 22 years, Dee has been involved in the community in various different ways and projects.

She is a Parent Governor, Community Governor, holds International Women's Day and International Men's Day events, as well as Health & Wellbeing events. Dee also hosts the Luton Black Film Club.

Dee is the founder of Simply Deez Events, RealTalk with Simply Deez, and the #LifeInnaLockdown weekly Zoom.

For Dee, heaven is a glass of Stones Ginger Wine and a bag of sweet 'n' salty popcorn.

She feels truly blessed to live her life, as tomorrow is not promised. Dee grabs life with both hands and sees where the journey takes her!

SIMPLY DEEZ EVENTS

Making it happen ◆ For you.

www.simplydeezeventscic.com

Life Inna Lockdown 2020
Behind Closed Doors
Sponsored by

www.marciampublishing.com

Printed in Poland
by Amazon Fulfillment
Poland Sp. z o.o., Wrocław

61183504R00090